Prospect to Profit

Joseph Marchese
Prospect to Profit

Published by Spines
ISBN: 979-8-89691-167-8

Prospect to Profit

A Salespersons Step by Step Guide

Joe Marchese

Contents

INTRODUCTION

In today's rapidly changing sales environment, a forever open mind is essential for success. Gone are the days of traditional sales tactics and one-size-fits-all approaches. Customers are more informed than ever, and they now seek partners who can solve their problems and enhance their offerings.

What worked in the past may not work today. The sales environment has evolved significantly, and what was effective a few years ago may no longer be relevant. It's crucial to adapt to changing customer needs and preferences and continuously learn new strategies.

To survive and dominate in today's cutthroat sales landscape, sales professionals and managers must adopt a relentless "Great White Shark" mentality. This means shifting from a product-focused approach to a predatory one, relentlessly hunting down opportunities and devouring the competition. This requires extreme sales activity, unwavering accountability, and a constant hunger for knowledge and adaptation. All the while, they must maintain a professional demeanor and deliver exceptional customer experiences.

Are you and your team prepared for this transformation? Are you training, practicing, and really holding yourselves accountable for sales activity that's professionally aggressive while delivering customer-centric solutions? If not, it's time to act. The competition is fierce, and those who do not adapt will be left behind.

Remember: As a Salesperson, you are in FULL CONTROL OF YOUR INCOME and your success depends on your mindset. You must decide to start EVERY DAY with a GREAT WHITE SHARK MENTALITY. By embracing a growth mindset and perfecting the skills you will learn in this book, you will continuously be honing your skills, and producing HIGH weekly sales activity. You WILL position yourself for long-term success to sustain In today's shark-infested waters.

Are you ready to check-in on and revolutionize your sales approach? Discover how to survive and thrive in today's competitive environment by adopting a problem-solving mindset, embracing continuous learning, and providing exceptional customer experiences. *"Prospect to Profit"* equips you with a step-by-step process with the tools and strategies needed to achieve lasting success. Learn this process, repeat it every day with every customer interaction and I promise you your results will shock you...

Joe Marchese

Step 1

Mindset: A Forever Open Mind

In the fast-paced world of sales, it's easy to fall into a routine and become complacent. Even seasoned professionals can find themselves stuck in a rut, forgetting the fundamental principles that drive success.

Have you ever attended a training session and felt a spark of inspiration? Perhaps you learned a new technique or gained a fresh perspective that resonated deeply. But as you returned to your daily routine, did that enthusiasm fade? Did those newfound insights get lost in the shuffle?

The truth is many salespeople and managers struggle with this. They know what they *should* do, but the demands of their jobs can make it difficult to consistently apply those principles. This is where having a **forever open mind** becomes crucial.

To achieve lasting success, you must be willing to challenge yourself and current assumptions, question your current practices, embrace new ideas and be willing to change the habits that aren't making you money. Even if you've been in the industry for years, there's always something to learn.

Prospect to Profit explains concepts that require a growth mindset and provides practical steps you can take to break free from limiting beliefs and adopt a more open-minded approach to sales.

Key Points to Remember:

- **The importance of a growth mindset:** Understand why a willingness to learn and adapt is essential for success.
- **Common pitfalls:** Recognize the obstacles that can hinder your ability to keep an open mind.
- **Strategies for overcoming challenges:** Discover practical techniques to break free from limiting beliefs and embrace new ideas.

You'll be introduced to the tools and insights needed to cultivate a forever open mind and unlock your full potential as a GREAT WHITE SHARK sales professional.

Overcoming the Habit Trap:

One of the biggest challenges to keeping an open mind is the power of habit. Our brains are wired to seek efficiency and habits can become deeply ingrained. When we're faced with a new idea or approach, our brains often resist change, clinging to familiar patterns.

Here are some strategies to break free from the habit trap:

1. **Conscious Awareness:** The first step is to become aware of your habits. Pay attention to your daily routines and find areas where you might be stuck in a rut.
2. **Challenge Assumptions:** Question your beliefs and assumptions about sales. Are there any limiting beliefs

that might be holding you back? **Example** – "I don't want to sound scripted…" **or** "Sitting in a room making prospecting calls is not the best use of my time…"

3. **Experimentation:** Be willing to try new things. Step outside of your comfort zone and explore different approaches. **Tip** – Don't try to change too many things at one time, but experiment with an urgency to implement.
4. **Continuous Learning:** Make learning a priority. Stay up to date on industry trends, attend workshops, and read books on sales and PRACTICE.
5. **Seek Feedback:** Ask for feedback from your colleagues, manager, and customers. This can help you find areas for improvement and gain new perspectives.

By actively working to overcome the habit trap, you can free your mind to embrace new ideas and approaches.

Building a Growth Mindset:

A growth mindset is essential for keeping an open mind. People with a growth mindset believe that their abilities can be developed through dedication and hard work; they see challenges as opportunities for growth, rather than as setbacks and lastly, they monitor their sales activity to ensure full potential and pivot when necessary.

Here are some strategies for cultivating a growth mindset:

1. **Focus on Progress:** Instead of focusing on perfection, celebrate your progress and learn from your mistakes. Implement new strategies.
2. **Identify Challenges:** View challenges as opportunities to learn and grow.

3. **Share your weekly goals:** When others are aware of what you're trying to achieve, your accountability will skyrocket for fear of underachieving and letting others down.
4. **Learn from Others:** Look for mentors and role models who inspire you.
5. **Practice Perseverance:** Don't give up when faced with setbacks. Persevere and keep pushing forward.

By developing a growth mindset, you will be better equipped to overcome challenges, embrace latest ideas, and achieve your goals.

A forever open mind is essential for success in sales. By breaking free from the habit trap and cultivating a growth mindset, you can position yourself for long-term success. Remember, there is always something to learn, and the willingness to adapt and grow is what sets the tremendously successful salespeople apart.

LOOKING YOURSELF IN THE MIRROR: SELF-ASSESSMENT FOR SALES SUCCESS

As a salesperson, you eat what you kill; you're the driving force behind your own success. While external factors like market conditions and company support play a role, your ultimate performance depends on your mindset, skills, and habits.

It's time to take a moment to look yourself in the mirror and honestly assess your current state. Are you truly operating at your full potential? Are you making the most of every opportunity?

Here are some key areas to consider when adapting to the Great White Shark Mentality:

Mindset:

- **Growth mindset:** Do you truly view challenges as opportunities for growth, or do you shy away from them?
- **Open-mindedness:** Are you receptive to new ideas and willing to adapt or, in some cases, totally change your approach?
- **Resilience:** How do you handle setbacks and failures? Do you bounce back quickly or let them discourage you?

Skills:

- **Product knowledge:** Do you have a deep understanding of your products or services?
- **Sales techniques:** Are you proficient in various sales methodologies? Do you practice and can you apply them effectively?
- **Communication:** Do you communicate clearly, confidently, and persuasively? Do you check in with your manager weekly and communicate your goals?

Habits:

- **Time management:** Are you efficient with your time and territory and able to prioritize tasks effectively?
- **Prospecting:** Are you consistently hunting for and generating new leads? Are you using the tools to generate leads that your company may provide you with? Are you nurturing relationships with potential and existing customers? Are you asking for referrals from every interaction?

- **Follow-up:** Do you follow up with prospects and customers in a timely and persistent manner?

Self-Reflection Questions:

- **Am I consistently striving to improve my skills and knowledge?**
- **Do I take responsibility for my own success, or do I blame external factors?**
- **Do I analyze my weekly activity and strive to improve?**
- **Am I willing to step outside of my comfort zone and try new things?**
- **Do I have a clear understanding of my strengths and weaknesses?**
- **Am I actively seeking feedback from my manager, colleagues, and customers?**

By honestly assessing these areas, you can identify areas where you can improve and take steps to become a more effective Great White Shark.

Remember, self-awareness is the first step towards self-improvement.

Take some time to reflect on your performance and make a commitment to continuous growth. The journey to sales success starts with looking at yourself in the mirror.

Let's look at what I feel is the very first step to achieving success in sales… Territory Management…

NOTES:

STEP 2

MASTERING YOUR TERRITORY: A STRATEGIC APPROACH

Many salespeople start their week without a clear plan of action, leading to wasted time and missed opportunities. Effective territory management is essential for maximizing productivity and achieving sales goals.

Key Strategies for Territory Management:

1. **Identify Hot Spots:** Pinpoint the areas or groups of potential prospects in your territory with the highest sales potential. Depending on the industry you work in, these may be regions, businesses or groups of people with a concentration of target customers, recent market activity, or upcoming events.
2. **Create a Weekly Schedule:** Develop a detailed weekly schedule that gives time in each hot spot. Consider the day of the week and time of day that are most likely to reach your target customers.
3. **Establish a Routine:** Consistency is key. Aim to visit the same areas on the same days of the week to build relationships with potential customers.

4. **Time Management:** Understand the time commitment needed for various sales activities, such as meetings, cold calls, and prospecting. Really break it down by time. **For Example:** If a prospecting call takes you an average of 1 minute 30 seconds, you can figure out how many calls you could make in a dedicated time frame. Take it to the next step and research the average closing ratio for prospecting for appointments over the phone. (PS – I looked it up for you, It's a **20% close ratio**. So, in the US, **10** calls should yield you **2** appointments) Let's take it even one step deeper. That means if you have a goal of 10 customer meetings this week, it will take you approximately 50 calls to achieve your goal. This will help you distribute your time effectively. **Note:** This deep dive into the numbers above would be considered a **Great White Shark** mentality.
5. **Optimize Your Route:** Plan your route to minimize travel time and maximize productivity. Consider using mapping software to optimize your route and estimate travel times.
6. **Prioritize Your Territory:** Visit the farthest part of your territory earlier in the week to maximize your time and reduce the stress of working in the farthest part of your territory early in the week.

By implementing these strategies, you can refine your territory management, improve your efficiency, and increase your chances of sales success.

Overcoming Challenges in Territory Management

Even with the best-laid plans, challenges can arise in territory management. Here are some common obstacles and strategies to overcome them:

- **Unexpected Changes:** Be prepared for unexpected changes, such as customer cancellations, traffic delays, or scheduled meetings running longer than expected. Stay flexible and be ready to adjust your schedule as needed. However, **prioritize your scheduled appointments** and avoid unnecessary disruptions. Remember, not every customer call is an emergency. If possible, reschedule or postpone less urgent requests without compromising your overall productivity.
- **Overwhelming Territory:** If your territory is too large to cover effectively, consider asking for help from your manager or exploring options for territory realignment.
- **Limited Resources:** If you're working with limited resources, prioritize your activities and focus on the most productive tasks.

What do I mean by limited resources? It means that a salesperson has a finite amount of time, energy, or potential leads available, and they mismanage or exhaust those resources early in the week; they won't have enough left to effectively pursue sales opportunities throughout the remaining days, potentially causing their sales performance to decline significantly.

- **Time Management:** Effective time management is essential for overcoming challenges in territory management. Use tools like calendars, planners or company CRM to stay organized and prioritize your tasks.
- **Customer Segmentation:** Segment your customers based on factors like revenue potential and engagement level. This can help you prioritize your time and focus on the most valuable accounts.
- **Lack of Motivation:** Stay motivated by setting

achievable goals, celebrating your successes, and seeking support from your colleagues or manager.

By addressing these challenges proactively, you can improve your territory management effectiveness and achieve your sales goals.

Leveraging Technology for Efficiency:

Technology can be a valuable tool for territory management. Consider using the following tools:

- **CRM Software:** A customer relationship management (CRM) system can help you track customer interactions, manage your pipeline, and analyze your sales performance.
- **Mapping Software:** Use mapping software to plan your routes, estimate travel times, and visualize your territory.
- **Mobile Apps:** There are many mobile apps available that can help you stay organized, manage your schedule, and track your sales activities.

Building Relationships with Key Stakeholders:

Building relationships with key stakeholders in your territory can be beneficial for your sales success. Consider reaching out and scheduling time as frequently as needed to share ideas.

- **Industry Associations:** Connect with industry associations to network with potential customers for possible sales and stay updated on industry trends to deliver business expertise in your weekly scheduled meetings.
- **Local Chambers of Commerce:** Join local chambers of commerce and attend meetings to build relationships

with other businesses in your area. These activities could possibly be during your personal time hours, just remember, Great White Sharks NEVER pass up a meal.

- **Community Leaders:** Develop relationships with community leaders to gain insights into local needs and opportunities.

By addressing challenges, using technology, and building relationships, you can effectively manage your territory and achieve your sales goals.

The Power of Territory Management:

Effective territory management is not just a strategy; it's a mindset. As a salesperson, you are the driver of your own success. The effort you put into planning and executing your territory strategy will directly affect your income.

NOTES:

Step 3

The Four Levels of Effort

To truly excel in sales, you must first confront the harsh reality of your current performance. By honestly assessing your activity level, you can identify areas for improvement and take decisive action to elevate your game.

The Four Levels of Effort provide a framework for self-evaluation. Each level represents a different approach to sales, with varying degrees of effectiveness. By understanding where you currently stand, you can take the necessary steps to transform yourself into an Apex Predator.

So, take a moment to reflect on your habits, your mindset, and your results. Are you a passive observer or an active hunter? Are you content with mediocrity or driven by a relentless pursuit of excellence? The choice is yours.

Shark-Bait Status	Activity	Impact
	**Passive Approach:** You rely heavily on referrals and inbound leads, taking a passive approach to sales. **Lack of Planning:** You have no structured sales plan or strategy, and you often work without a clear direction. **Poor Time Management:** You waste time on unproductive activities, such as excessive socializing or browsing the internet. **Fear of Rejection:** You avoid making cold calls and other proactive sales activities due to fear of rejection.	**LOW Sales Volume** Stagnant sales pipeline, missed opportunities, and a reputation as a non-performer. Your lack of proactive effort is directly impacting your income and hindering your career growth. You're essentially a bystander in a high-stakes game.

To escape the "Shark Bait" status, you must adopt a more proactive and aggressive approach. Set clear goals, develop a strong sales plan, and consistently execute your strategy. Don't be afraid to step outside of your comfort zone and take calculated risks.

The Hesitant Shark	Activity	Impact
	Sporadic Prospecting: You engage in occasional prospecting efforts, but they lack consistency and focus. **Limited Territory Planning:** You have a basic understanding of your territory, but you don't have a well-defined strategy for targeting and prioritizing opportunities. **Difficulty with Gatekeepers:** You often struggle to connect with decision-makers, as you lack the skills and confidence to navigate gatekeepers effectively. **Inconsistent Performance:** Your sales results are inconsistent, with periods of strong performance followed by periods of stagnation.	**Moderate Sales Volume** Inconsistent performance, missed quotas, and a lack of strategic focus. Your half-hearted efforts are limiting your potential. You're nibbling at the edges instead of going for the kill. It's time to stop treading water and start swimming with purpose.

To transform yourself from a Hesitant Shark to a more formidable predator, you need to develop a more proactive and disciplined approach. Focus on building strong relationships, honing your communication skills, and consistently executing your sales plan.

The Occasional Threat	Activity	Impact
	**Inconsistent Effort:** You're making some progress, but your efforts are sporadic. You need to develop a more consistent and disciplined approach. **Basic Territory Management:** You have a general understanding of your territory, but your planning could be more strategic. **Limited Gatekeeper Handling:** You can sometimes navigate gatekeepers, but you need to improve your skills to consistently gain access to decision-makers. **Occasional Strong Pitches:** You deliver strong pitches from time to time, but you need to refine your messaging and delivery to be more impactful.	**Increasing Sales Volume** You're making progress, but you're not capitalizing on your full potential. Your inconsistent approach is limiting your ability to dominate your territory. It's time to sharpen your skills, optimize your strategy, and become a true force in the market.

It's time to elevate your game. By committing to a more consistent and strategic approach, you can transform yourself from an "Occasional Threat" to a formidable force in the sales world.

The APEX PREDATOR	Activity	Impact
	Relentless Pursuit: Consistently seek out new opportunities. Your territory is your hunting ground, and you must scour it relentlessly. **Strategic Planning:** Develop a detailed plan for every interaction. Anticipate objections, prepare compelling responses, and always have a clear next step. **Masterful Communication:** Hone your communication skills. Your ability to articulate value, build rapport, and influence decision-makers is crucial. **Leadership by Example:** Inspire your peers with your drive and determination. Share your knowledge and experience and empower others to succeed. **Unwavering Focus:** Stay laser-focused on your goals. Block out distractions, prioritize tasks, and maintain a relentless pursuit of excellence.	**High Sales Volume** You're a dominant force in the market, consistently exceeding expectations. Your relentless pursuit of excellence has established you as a top performer. You're not just closing deals; you're shaping the future of the business. Keep pushing the limits and maintaining your position as the ultimate sales professional.

The Apex Predator is the epitome of sales excellence. They are relentlessly proactive, meticulously planning their every move. Their expert communication skills allow them to navigate complex sales cycles with ease, securing high-value deals. They inspire and motivate their peers, setting the standard for success. Their consistent performance and strategic thinking make them indispensable to the organization.

Now that you've identified your current activity level, it's time to take decisive action. Whether you're a Shark Bait, a Hesitant Shark, an Occasional Threat, or an Apex Predator, there's always room for improvement. By embracing the principles of empowerment, responsibility, proactivity, and accountability, you can elevate your sales performance and achieve your career goals. Remember, the sales world is a competitive arena. To succeed, you must be relentless, strategic, and always striving for excellence.

Key Principles for Success:

1. **Unleash Your Inner Apex Predator:** Take ownership of your career and embrace a relentless pursuit of excellence. Your actions define your destiny.
2. **Dominate Your Territory:** Be proactive in managing your territory, hunting down opportunities, and closing deals. Remember, the sales arena is your hunting ground.
3. **Master the Art of Persuasion:** Hone your communication skills and develop the ability to influence decision-makers. Your words are your weapons, use them wisely.
4. **Lead by Example:** Share your goals with others and inspire your peers. Your commitment to excellence will motivate those around you.

By embodying these principles and implementing the strategies outlined in this chapter, you can rise to the top of the sales world. Remember, the future is yours to shape.

NOTES:

Step 4

Phone Prospecting: The Art of the Call

Effective phone prospecting is a vital skill for any salesperson. It allows you to reach out to potential customers, generate leads, and schedule valuable meetings.

Key Strategies for Phone Prospecting:

1. **Dedicated Time: Set aside dedicated time** each week for phone prospecting, such as two 2-hour sessions.
2. **Goal-Oriented:** Remember that the **goal of phone prospecting is to schedule meetings**, not just make calls.
3. **Preparation: Prepare lists of potential prospects prior to your scheduled prospecting time** using your CRM, company database, and other resources. Try not to prepare lists during this scheduled valuable time.
4. **Gatekeeper Strategies: Develop strategies to bypass gatekeepers,** such as calling at off-peak times or targeting specific departments.
5. **Interest-Capturing Statements: Craft compelling**

statements that highlight a potential benefit or solution for the prospect.

6. **Make Sure Your Interest-Capturing Statement is Solution-Focused:** Articulate how your company can address the prospect's needs or challenge that was mentioned in the interest-capturing statement.
7. **Overcoming Objections: Expect, address and EMPATHISE common objections** to scheduling a meeting. **Note:** I recommend and have had incredible results using the **Feel, Felt, Found** method. It's a universal technique that can be applied to almost any scenario. It's the perfect response to a large majority of phone objections. It helps you foster a connection by relating to their problem. (you will see an example coming up)
8. **Scheduling Flexibility:** Offer the prospect multiple (2) meeting times to accommodate their schedule.

Interest-Capturing Statement

- An Interest Capturing Statement is a concise, compelling statement (short and concise) that captures your prospective customers' attention and sparks their curiosity about your offering. It's essentially a "hook" that draws them in and makes them want to hear more.

Example:

- "Hi! Mr. or Mrs. Prospect, this is (Your Name) from (Your Company). Thank you for taking my call.

Interest-Capturing Statement

- " I'm reaching out because companies like yourself have been experiencing (**Enter an issue or problem that mutable companies/people experience).** I believe our (product/service) can help you address (the specific need or challenge)."

Addressing Objections While Phone Prospecting:

- **Customer Objection #1:** *"I've heard of your company and had always assumed you were an expensive option."*
    - **Salesperson Response:** "I understand why you might **Feel** that way, other clients had **Felt** the same way initially, but what they **Found** after meeting with me was that we weren't expensive compared to the possible outcomes without implementing our (Product/Service). I'd like to discuss how our (Product/Service) can help you achieve your goals."
    - **Immediately continue without hesitation by saying...**
    - I'm going to be in that area tomorrow at 1 or Friday at 3; which time works best for you?

Note: Be prepared for a possible second objection...

- **Customer Objection #2:** *"You know what, that sounds interesting, I'd like to learn more about your company, so why don't you just send me some information..."*
    - **Salesperson Response: "That's Exactly why we need to meet**, during our meeting, I'll be able to ask some questions and narrow down some of the most useful (Products/Services) that I can offer

you that will bring you the most benefits. Let's definitely do that in person, I'm going to be in that area tomorrow at 1 or Friday at 3; which time works best for you?"

- **Customer Response:** *"Ok, well, that sounds fair, let's do Friday at 3".*

Handling the Second Objection:

When a prospect expresses a need for more information, consider using the phrase, "That's exactly why we need to meet." This approach can be employed independently or in conjunction with the Feel, Felt, Found technique.

By scheduling an in-person meeting, you can effectively articulate how your company aligns with the prospect's specific requirements and demonstrate your value proposition.

Always offer a few times to meet:

This method demonstrates persistence and value by showing that you're invested in their needs and willing to work with their schedule. It also places the customer in control and gives them a choice. Not to mention it lets the prospect know that you're busy, too.

Pack Prospecting: A Collaborative Approach

Pack prospecting is a powerful technique that involves teaming up with other salespeople to share best practices, motivate each other, and increase productivity. By working together, you can create a healthy competitive environment and achieve greater success.

Benefits of Pack Prospecting:

- **Increased Motivation:** Collaborating with others can boost your motivation and make phone prospecting more enjoyable.
- **Shared Knowledge:** Learn from the experiences and techniques of your fellow salespeople.
- **Accountability:** Having accountability partners can help you stay focused and committed to your goals.
- **Enhanced Productivity:** By working together, you can increase your overall productivity and achieve more in less time.

Tips for Effective Pack Prospecting:

- **Set Clear Goals:** Set up specific goals for your pack prospecting sessions, such as the number of calls to make or appointments to schedule.
- **Create a Positive Atmosphere:** Foster a supportive and encouraging environment where everyone feels comfortable sharing their experiences.
- **Provide and Accept Feedback:** Offer constructive feedback to your teammates to help them improve their skills.
- **Celebrate Success:** Recognize and celebrate the achievements of your team members to support high morale.

By incorporating pack prospecting into your phone prospecting strategy, you can enhance your effectiveness, boost your motivation, and achieve greater success.

NOTES:

Step 5

Making a Lasting Impression: The Power of the Opening

Your first impression can have a significant impact on the outcome of a sales meeting. By starting the meeting with a strong and professional opening, you can show credibility, gain the customer's attention, and set the tone for a successful interaction.

Key Elements of a Powerful Opening:

1. **Professionalism:** Arrive on time, dress appropriately, and maintain a professional demeanor.
2. **Introduction:** Clearly say your name company, hand them your card and state the purpose of the meeting.
3. **Agenda:** Provide a brief overview of the topics you plan to discuss.
4. **Customer Focus:** Make it clear that the meeting is about the customer's needs and challenges.
5. **Ensure everyone necessary is in attendance:** When you open a meeting professionally and state your purpose, sometimes the decision maker will decide to involve other people who need to be present for the

meeting. **Note:** This occurs more frequently than you might imagine. Decision-makers are inundated with sales calls daily. By presenting yourself professionally from the outset, you can pique their interest and encourage them to involve others in the conversation. This significant indicator positions you as a knowledgeable and valuable business partner.

6. **Active Listening:** Show that you're genuinely interested in understanding the customer's perspective. Lean in and sit with a professional posture.
7. **Call to Action:** Clearly state your desired outcome, such as scheduling a follow-up meeting or discussing the next steps to move forward today.

Quick tip - At the end of your powerful opening, I recommend to EXPLICITLY state that you are there today to earn their business, as it sets clear expectations, demonstrates transparency and positions you as someone who is actively seeking to prove their value to the customer.

Avoid Common Pitfalls:

- **Excessive Self-Promotion:** Don't focus solely on your company or products.
- **Passive Listening:** Avoid simply nodding along while the customer speaks.
- **Lack of Direction:** Have a clear agenda and purpose for the meeting.
- **Closing Too Soon:** Don't rush to close the deal before you've fully understood the customer's needs and have been able to bring a valuable solution to their challenges.

Example of a Powerful Opening

"Good morning, Mr. Smith. I'm (Your Name) from (Your Company). Thank you for taking the time to meet with me today. As we discussed on the phone, I'm confident that our (Product/Service) can help you (restate the specific benefit or solution).

To better understand your needs, I'll begin by asking a few questions. Then, I'll outline how our company can support your goals and address your challenges.

Before we proceed, I want to ensure that everyone who would benefit from this discussion is present. Is there anyone else who should join our meeting today?

Now that we have everyone here let's briefly review the topics we'll be discussing: (Topic 1), (Topic 2), and (Topic 3). I'm particularly interested in learning more about your specific goals and challenges around these topics. After our discussion, I'll be happy to answer any questions you may have and provide more details about our solution.

If everything aligns with your needs, I'll be asking for your business at the end of our meeting. How does that sound?

This opening is strong and professional. It clearly introduces the purpose of the meeting, sets expectations, and ensures all relevant stakeholders are involved.

By following these guidelines, you can create a powerful opening that will leave a lasting impression and position you for success.

NOTES:

Step 6

Active Listening and Questioning: Uncovering Customer Needs

Active listening and skillful questioning are paramount in successful sales interactions. Immediately following your meeting's opening, initiate a dialogue by asking insightful and probing questions. This phase is crucial to a successful sales interaction as you actively seek to uncover their underlying needs and challenges. Take thorough notes while carefully listening to the customer's responses. This will provide valuable information that you can leverage throughout the meeting. By properly executing this step, you'll gain valuable insights that will guide your sales strategy and ultimately increase your chances of closing the deal.

Effective Questioning Techniques:

1. Open-Ended Questions:

Encourage the customer to provide detailed and thoughtful answers by asking open-ended questions that begin with "what," "how," "why," or "could."

Examples:

- "What are your biggest challenges in [specific area]?"
- "How do you currently address [specific need]?"

• "Why is [specific goal] important to you?"

• "Could you tell me more about your experience with [previous solutions]?"

2. Probing Questions:

Follow up on the customer's responses to delve deeper into their thoughts and feelings.

Examples:

• "Can you elaborate on that?"

• "What are the specific consequences of [the issue]?"

• "How does that make you feel?"

• "What are your concerns about [the proposed solution]?"

3. Hypothetical Questions:

Ask questions that explore potential scenarios or outcomes.

Examples:

• "If you could wave a magic wand, how would you solve this problem?"

• "What would success look like in this situation?"

• "How would your life/business be different if [the problem were solved]?"

• "What are the potential risks and rewards of [a particular course of action]?"

4. Impact Questions:

Ask questions that focus on the impact of the customer's challenges on their business or personal life.

Examples:

• "How is this issue impacting your productivity?"

• "What are the financial implications of this problem?"

• "How is this affecting your team morale?"

• "How is this impacting your ability to achieve your goals?"

By incorporating these questioning techniques and examples, you can effectively engage customers in a meaningful conversation, uncover their true needs, and build stronger relationships.

Active Listening Tips:

1. **Maintain Eye Contact:** Show that you're engaged and interested in the conversation.
2. **Use Verbal Cues:** Use verbal cues to show that you're listening and understanding.
   - Examples of verbal cues are, "I see," "I got it," "That makes sense," and "Tell me more."
3. **Paraphrase:** Restate the customer's main points to ensure that you've understood correctly.
4. **Avoid Interrupting:** Let the customer finish speaking before responding.
5. **Take Notes:** Jot down key points to reference later in the conversation.

Analyzing Customer Responses:

As you listen to the customer's responses, pay attention to their emotions, concerns, and priorities. Look for clues that show their underlying needs or pain points. These insights will help you tailor your presentation and address the customer's specific concerns.

Remember: The goal of active listening and questioning is to build rapport, understand the customer's perspective, and find opportunities to provide value. By effectively engaging with the customer, you can position yourself as a trusted advisor and increase your chances of closing the sale.

Helpful tip: Dig Deeper

Once you have found a challenge or a need, **do not stop questioning.** Continue to probe and explore the issue to gain a deeper understanding of its impact. Help the customer realize the "unrealized" effects that this challenge is having on their business and the broader organization.

By digging deeper, you can uncover more needs or concerns that the customer may not have initially found. This will allow you to tailor your solution more effectively and show your expertise. This will be reviewed more in the next chapter.

NOTES:

STEP 7

THE POWER OF VISUALS: BRING THE CHALLENGE TO LIFE

You have uncovered the challenge that the customer needs to address! You spent lots of time asking great questions that uncovered some unrealized effects on the customer, his team and the business. LET'S go even deeper and bring it to life! But first, it's important for me to remind you that in today's fast-paced world, capturing and keeping your audience's attention is crucial. Especially when preparing your customers to see the value in what you offer, while verbal explanations are valuable, incorporating visuals can significantly enhance your message's impact and memorability. Studies have shown that using visuals can increase information retention by up to 65%.

Benefits of Using Visuals:

- **Enhanced Engagement:** Visuals can make your presentation more engaging and interesting.
- **Improved Retention:** Visuals can help your audience remember key points more effectively.
- **Clarity and Understanding:** Visuals can clarify

complex concepts and make your message easier to understand.

- **Persuasion:** Visuals can be a powerful tool for persuasion, as they can evoke emotions and create a lasting impression.

Types of Visuals:

- **Charts and Graphs:** Use charts and graphs to present data and trends in a clear and concise manner.
- **Diagrams:** Create diagrams to illustrate complex concepts or processes.
- **Images:** Use images to represent ideas, products, or services.
- **Videos:** Incorporate videos to show products, share testimonials, or tell stories.

Example #1 of Using Visuals in a Sales Presentation:

Scenario: You are a salesperson presenting to a construction company that is experiencing delays due to unreliable service providers.

Visual: Create a simple chart or simply use your notebook, showing the cost of:

- **Lost productivity:** Jobsite downtime. Calculate the amount the job site downtime is costing them and circle it right in front of them.
- **Decreased customer satisfaction:** Possible need to give a discount. Calculate what giving a discount could look like and multiply that by the percentage of their customers this challenge could be affecting. Circle the amount.

- **Reputational damage caused by these delays:** Loss of potential future jobs. Calculate a certain amount of lost business for the year and circle it in front of them.

By visually representing the monetary impact, you can make the problem more tangible and compelling.

Example #2 of Using Visuals in a Sales Presentation:

Scenario: You are a salesperson trying to convince a marketing team to invest in a new CRM system.

Visual: Create a simple chart comparing the current situation to the potential benefits of the new CRM system. The chart could include the following metrics:

- **Increased lead conversion rate:** Show a percentage increase and circle it in front of them.
- **Improved customer satisfaction:** Display a customer satisfaction rating before and after implementing the CRM. Draw an arrow pointing up to the sky to show the satisfaction rate going up.
- **Reduced administrative time:** Present a comparison of time spent on administrative tasks before and after. Write down OVERTIME and calculate the amount of overspending on wages. Write it down and underline it.
- **Enhanced sales team collaboration:** Highlight improved communication and teamwork. Draw a HUGE happy face showing the happy faces due to better communication.

These are just a few of the many examples you could use. By visually representing these benefits, you can make a compelling case for the new CRM system and show its value to the marketing team.

Remember: The key to effective visual communication is to use visuals that are relevant, clear, and easy to understand. Avoid overwhelming your audience with too much information or using visuals that are difficult to interpret.

Important Tip: Positively Frame the Amount Revealed

When presenting the financial or operational impact of a challenge, it's essential to frame the information in a way that creates a sense of urgency without pressuring the customer. Focus on highlighting the potential benefits of addressing the issue and the negative consequences of inaction.

Here are some tips for positively framing the amount revealed:

- **Highlight the Opportunity:** Emphasize the potential for growth, improvement, or cost savings that can be achieved by addressing the challenge.
- **Use Positive Language:** Avoid using negative or alarmist language that could alienate the customer.
- **Focus on the Future:** Paint a picture of a brighter future where the challenge has been resolved.
- **Create a Sense of Urgency:** Gently remind the customer of the time-sensitive nature of the issue.

By positively framing the amount revealed, you can encourage the customer to consider the consequences of inaction and motivate them to take the next step.

NOTES:

Step 8

Setting the Stage: Preparing for the Solution Presentation

Before presenting your product or service, it's essential to verify that the customer has acknowledged the problem, it's unrealized cost that you just brought to life and is committed to finding a solution. This step is crucial for ensuring that your efforts are aligned with the customer's needs and goals.

Script Example: Conditional Commitment #1

Salesperson: (Mr. or Mrs. Customer) Do you agree that we've uncovered some challenges and shed some light on the approximate dollar amount it's costing you?

Customer: Yes! Thank you! Your approach today has been very helpful. I now realize the full impact these issues are having on the business.

Salesperson: That's great! One other thing: **if the solutions I present make sense and prove to be an immediate benefit, are you committed to resolving the challenge and giving me an opportunity to earn your business today?**

NOTE – The statement above is called a **Conditional Commitment #1 -** It's the very first step in the closing process. You're confirming that you have successfully brought a heightened awareness to a challenge and confirming that they want to make a change.

Suppose the customer's head is nodding yes throughout this part of the conversation and they respond with a yes to your conditional commitment questions. In that case, your possibility of selling this customer is **HIGH.**

Customer: Yes! I'm very interested in hearing about your potential solutions.

Salesperson: Great! Let's jump in...

By using this script, you can effectively **verify** the customer's understanding of the problem and their willingness to consider alternative solutions.

Transitioning to the Solution Presentation:

Once you've verified the customer's understanding of the problem and their commitment to finding a solution, it's time to transition into your product or service presentation. Here are some tips for making a smooth transition:

- **Recap Key Points:** Briefly summarize the main points discussed so far in the meeting.
- **Transition Statement:** Use a transition statement to bridge the gap between the problem and the solution. For example, you could say, **"Now that we've identified the challenges you're facing, I'd like to introduce our solution."**
- **Highlight Relevance:** Emphasize how your product or service directly addresses the customer's specific needs and challenges.
- **Build Excitement:** Create anticipation and excitement about the potential benefits of your solution.

It will sound something like this:

Salesperson: Mr. or Mrs. Customer, to summarize, (insert the challenge) is an overall larger problem than you were originally aware of. And you agree that it's affecting you and your business. Now that we've isolated the challenge, I'd like to directly address the issue and introduce our solution...

By following these steps, you can effectively transition from the problem-solving phase to the solution presentation phase of the sales process.

NOTES:

STEP 9

PRESENTING THE SOLUTION: TAILORING YOUR PROPOSITION

Once you've established the customer's needs, commitment and interest in hearing what you have to offer, it's time to present your solution.

Choose the Relevant Value Proposition and avoid overwhelming the customer with too many value propositions. Select the one or two of your solutions that most effectively address the specific challenge they've named.

Explain the Solution with a 3-step approach: Introduce the solution, clearly explain how your solution works and what it will do to help the customer. Be sure to stay specific to the challenge revealed and avoid overselling your solution. Then, Highlight the Benefits by Emphasizing the tangible and intangible benefits that the customer will experience.

3 Steps Solution Presentation: Follow this script.

Step 1: Introduction to the Solution: Together, we've found that your (Challenge) is causing (State the Specific consequence you brought to life). Our Solution that I feel is the best is (Name your Value Proposition)

Step 2: Functions of the Solution: It's designed to address your challenge by (Provide a clear and concise explanation of how your solution works and what it will do)

Note: List some of the solutions results. Jot them down to encourage a better understanding. Just keep it relevant to solving the challenge at hand.

Step 3: Benefits and Advantages of elevating the challenge: By implementing our solution, you will experience the following benefits:

Note: List the benefits and write them down again in front of the customer.

[Benefit 1]

[Benefit 2]

[Benefit 3]

It's now time for Conditional Commitment #2: Ask for a tentative commitment to move forward. For example, you could say,

Salesperson: Mr. Customer, does this make sense? Do you see how this could help you with the challenge we discussed? Could you see yourself making this valuable investment in me and my company today?"

Customer: Yes, this would be a huge win for the business and me. It sounds like that could really help our situation.

Important Note: Conditional Commitment #2 - If the customer's head is nodding yes throughout this part of the conversation, they are smiling, have great eye contact and are leaning in responding with a **yes** to your second conditional commitment question, your possibility of selling this customer is **VERY HIGH. They have reached what I call THE POINT OF ACTIVATION.**

The point of activation is when a customer fully understands the value of what you are offering. The 2 POSITIVE Conditional Commitments that you received have prepared them for this moment. The odds of them saying yes at this very moment are the highest they will ever be.

You must be able to identify this moment and be confident in asking for the business and at FULL PRICE.

Remember: Tailor your solution presentation to the specific needs and interests reviewed in the meeting with the customer. Use clear and concise language and give concrete examples to illustrate the benefits of your solution. Also, BE SURE YOU GET REALLY GOOD AT IDENTIFYING **THE POINT OF ACTIVATION.**

Clues that the Customer has reached The Point of Activation

Verbal Clues	Non-Verbal Clues	Engagement
They will ask questions for deeper understanding.	Body Language: Leaning in, making eye contact, actively listening	Time Commitment: They are willing to dedicating time to future meetings
Listen for positive Language: "Interesting", "That's Valuable", "This could be a good fit"	Taking notes and jotting down points	Next Steps: They agree to a proposal / quote and face to face follow up meetings
They will openly discuss their budget	Facial Expressions: Smile, nodding yes and engaged in what you're saying	Introducing you to others: They are happy to introduce you to other people in the organization.
They express urgency with upcoming timeframes	Ignoring other calls.	They are willing to give you a referral.

NOTES:

Step 10

Addressing Any Remaining Concerns and Setting the Stage for the Profitable Close

Before discussing pricing, it's crucial to ensure that you've isolated the primary challenge that will seal the deal and that the customer has no other significant concerns. There's 1 sentence that will help you avoid any surprises or setbacks during the closing process. See below...

Script Example:

You: We've had a productive conversation today, and I'm confident that our solution can address the challenge we discussed.

Customer: Yes, I'm interested in moving forward with your company. I would like to discuss the cost of your service next.

You: That's great! I'm happy to hear you're interested in partnering with us. Before we dive into specifics on cost, I want to ensure that I have fully addressed your primary concern, which is (Reiterate the main challenge). **Is there anything else that might be a potential hurdle to getting started today?**

Customer: No, that's the last piece of the puzzle for me. I'm happy with everything we discussed today. I just need to understand the cost of the service and terms.

You: Great! I'm happy to discuss this with you. (Provide clear and transparent pricing information, including any relevant terms and conditions.)

Remember: By addressing any remaining concerns before discussing pricing, you can increase your chances of a successful close.

Additionally, it's essential to have all the necessary information to provide a correct and competitive quote.

Key Considerations for Clear Transparent Pricing:

- **Gather Detailed Information:** Collect all relevant information about the customer's needs, requirements, and preferences.
- **Understand Your Company's Costs:** Be knowledgeable about your company's costs associated with providing the product or service.
- **Decide Your Profit Margin:** Figure out the desired profit margin for your company.
- **Set Price Guardrails:** Set up clear guidelines for pricing decisions, including when to seek approval from your manager.

Ensure Accuracy: Even if you think you can provide a quote without extensive questioning, it's always a good practice to gather as much information as possible to avoid the need for revisions. Remember, a revised quote can diminish your credibility and damage the trust you've built with the customer.

Avoiding Price Revisions: To avoid the need for post-sale price revisions, ensure that your first quote is correct and comprehensive. Gather all necessary information upfront and double-check your calculations before presenting the quote.

Maintaining Confidence and Trust:

Even if you need to adjust the price, it's important to maintain your confidence and trustworthiness. Explain any changes clearly and transparently and avoid appearing hesitant or unsure.

Remember: By being well-prepared and confident in your pricing, you can increase your chances of closing the deal and securing a profitable sale.

The Importance of NOT Prematurely Discounting:

When presenting your price, it's essential to maintain confidence and avoid discounting your solution prematurely. Here are some reasons why:

- **Decision Already Made:** The customer may have already decided to move forward, and a discount might not be necessary to close the deal.
- **Limited Time or Options:** The customer may be under pressure to decide due to limited time or limited alternative choices.
- **Strong Value Proposition:** If you've effectively presented the value of your solution, the customer is at their Point of Activation and, in their excitement, may be willing to pay the full price.

Tip: If you don't ask, you don't get.

By maintaining confidence and avoiding unnecessary discounts, you can increase your chances of closing the deal at a profitable price.

NOTES:

Step 11

Closing the Deal: Securing the Commitment

Once you've addressed remaining concerns (if any) and gathered all essential information, you will have set the stage for closing, it's time to present the price and secure the customer's commitment.

Presenting the Price:

- **Be Clear, Concise and Confident:** State the price clearly and concisely, avoiding any ambiguity.
- **Be sure that the Specific Agreed Upon Value is Presented with the Price:** Present the price with the Specifics that the customer saw value in.
- **Address Concerns:** Be prepared to address any concerns the customer may have about the price.

Be Prepared to Handle Customer Reactions:

- **Stay Silent:** After presenting the price and the value the customer has agreed upon, they fully understand

and find value. Remain silent and allow the customer to process the information.

- **Address Objections:** If the customer raises objections, address them calmly and confidently.
- **Avoid Discounting Prematurely:** Unless absolutely necessary, avoid offering discounts without a clear justification.

Securing the Commitment:

- **Assume The Sale!!** Once the customer has shown their interest in moving forward, **Thank Them for The Business!**
- **Maintain Momentum:** Keep the conversation moving forward to avoid giving the customer time to second-guess their decision.
- **Transition to Next Steps:** If the customer agrees to move forward, immediately transition to the next steps, such as an introduction to another department and scheduling a follow-up meeting to ensure satisfaction after delivery of product or service.

Example of Closing the Deal:

Salesperson: (Be Clear, Concise and Confident) Alright, Mr. or Mrs. Customer, based on our discussion, the cost for (Product or Service) is ($Price). This price includes **(Specifics that the customer agreed were valuable).** Are you ready to move forward?

(Stay Silent)

Customer: Alright, that sounds about right. I have an immediate need for this solution and would like to implement it as soon as possible.

Salesperson: Thank you for your business! We can move quickly and implement this (or) deliver this as soon as possible.

(Maintain Momentum)

Salesperson: Next, I'd like to meet the person in accounts payable who would handle our account. I could introduce myself and give them my contact information, so if there are any questions, they have a face to a name. Also, let's set up a meeting today in our calendars after you experience our (Product or Service). I would like to ensure your satisfaction and that the benefits of using (Your Company Name) are everything we discussed. How does Tuesday the 5th at 1 pm or Thursday the 7th at 3 pm look for you as of now?

Customer: Good thinking, I get busy, setting a meeting up now would be best. Let's do Tuesday the 5$^{th.}$

Salesperson: One last thing: I would like to receive 5 referrals from you today from other people you know in the industry who would benefit from working with me.

Remember: Ask for referrals from EVERY CUSTOMER INTERACTION.

By following these steps and maintaining confidence throughout the closing process, you can increase your chances of securing the customer's commitment and closing the deal.

Avoid Leaving Deals on the Table:

One of the most common mistakes salespeople make is not asking for the business after presenting the price. This can lead to lost opportunities and decreased sales.

Reasons Why Salespeople Hesitate to Close:

- **Fear of Rejection:** Some salespeople may be afraid of being rejected or perceived as pushy.
- **Lack of Confidence:** A lack of confidence in their value proposition or their ability to close the deal can hinder salespeople's ability to ask for the commitment.

- **Overthinking:** Overthinking the situation or trying to predict every possible objection can lead to hesitation.

Strategies for Closing the Deal:

- **Maintain Confidence:** Believe in the value of your solution and your ability to close the deal.
- **Be Assertive:** Ask for the commitment directly and confidently, without being aggressive.
- **Address Objections:** Be prepared to address any objections the customer may raise.
- **Focus on Benefits:** Remind the customer of the benefits they will receive by moving forward with your solution.

QUICK TIME OUT

While the previous scenarios painted an ideal sales meeting, it's important to remember that your everyday interactions may vary. However, if there's one crucial takeaway from this book, it's **the power of consistent execution.** If you discover a successful sales approach, whether in this book or somewhere else, **stick with it** and **don't let distractions derail your progress**. By diligently following the scripts and processes outlined in this book, you'll build a strong foundation and become more equipped to handle different scenarios.

The Great White Shark mentality is about unwavering commitment to your approach. While you may need to adapt your strategy occasionally, sticking to the proven process will significantly increase your chances of success. Over time, you'll gain a deeper understanding of your customers' needs and anticipate their responses more effectively.

With a solid foundation in sales fundamentals and a consistent approach, you're well-prepared to tackle the next crucial

step: effective price negotiation. Let's explore strategies to confidently discuss pricing and secure favorable deals.

NOTES:

Step 12

Negotiating Price Effectively

One of the most common challenges in sales is negotiating price. However, with the right approach, you can effectively address price objections and secure a profitable deal.

Understanding Price Objections:

The price objection is often a result of the customer's perception of value. If you haven't effectively communicated the value of your solution, the customer may be hesitant to pay the full price.

Strategies for Handling Price Objections:

1. **Reiterate Value:** Remind the customer of the benefits they will receive from your solution and how it addresses their specific needs.
2. **Avoid Premature Discounts:** Don't offer discounts too quickly. Instead, use negotiation tactics (see below) to extract maximum value.

3. **Have a Negotiation Plan:** Develop a clear negotiation strategy, including the amount you're willing to discount and the conditions under which you'll offer a discount.
4. **Frame Discounts Strategically:** Consider offering discounts in a way that supports your perceived value. For example, you could offer a discount on a specific feature or add-on rather than discounting the entire product or service.

Discounting Tactics:

- **Reserve Discounts for Value-Added Features:** Offer discounts on additional features or services rather than discounting the base price.
- **Use Limited-Time Offers:** Create a sense of urgency by offering limited-time discounts or promotions.
- **Bundle Products or Services:** Offer discounts for purchasing multiple products or services together.
- **Give Discounts Strategically:** Believe it or not, how you give a discount will guide the customer to take the deal or not. See below.

Providing Discount to obtain the business today: A Strategic Approach

When you've successfully navigated the sales process and earned a customer's trust as a business expert, the way you handle discounts can significantly impact the relationship. A well-executed discount strategy can reinforce your position as a trusted advisor, while a misstep can undermine the value you've carefully cultivated.

Remember, your customer has reached this point because they firmly believe that your solutions will benefit them personally as well as their company. By strategically approaching discounts, you can further solidify this trust and strengthen your partnership.

Note: A key consideration is the number of opportunities you have to negotiate the price.

In many cases, you'll have only **three chances** to adjust the discount within your predetermined parameters. This aligns with the concept of **"knowing your guardrails,"** a strategy I teach that involves clear communication with your management team to establish acceptable discount levels without requiring constant approval.

Example Negotiation:

In the example below, you'll provide a full $200.00 discount. However, the focus is on ***how*** you arrive at the point you present the discount. Pay close attention to the strategies employed.

Salesperson: Mr. Customer, the price is $1,000, and that includes all the benefits (list them out) that we discussed today. (stay silent)

Customer: Well, it's a bit more than I anticipated.

Note: *First opportunity to give a discount.*

Strategy used: Reiterate what brought the customer to the Point of activation.

Salesperson: Let's review what you agreed upon was the long- and short-term benefits that we identified in today's meeting. (reiterate benefits)

Customer: Being that your price is a little over budget, I would need a higher approval, which might prolong me moving forward with you today. Is there any room at all for a discount?

Note: *Second opportunity to give a discount.*

Strategy used: Feel, Felt, Found.

Salesperson: I understand how you **feel**; other

customers **felt** the same way when I first presented the cost, but what they **found** was that in the long run, the benefits they experienced supported their business goals and gave them a better reputation in their business market resulting in happy customers and more business.

Customer: Yes, me AND my company would like the results we'll achieve by using your company, but I'm still a bit over budget.

Note: Final opportunity to give a discount.

Strategy used: Conditional Commitment & Asking for Referrals

Salesperson: If I give you a discount, will that ensure you move forward with me and my company today?

Customer: Yes! That will ensure we move forward with you today.

Salesperson: OK, I will discount the price by $200. One last thing: I would like to receive 5 referrals from you today of other people you know in the industry who would benefit from working with me. Do we have a Deal?

This example can be used in many different negotiation situations. The goal is to prolong the discount and take the time to reiterate the benefits prior to just giving your profit away.

NOTES:

STEP 13

NEXT STEP OBSESSED: THE POWER OF FOLLOW UP

Many salespeople focus solely on closing the deal and neglect the importance of post-sale follow-up. However, building strong relationships with your customers is essential for long-term success.

Why Follow-Up Matters:

- **Customer Satisfaction:** Regular follow-up shows your commitment to customer satisfaction and helps build trust.
- **Repeat Business:** Nurturing relationships can lead to repeat business and referrals.
- **Customer Insights:** Following up with customers can offer valuable insights into their needs and preferences.
- **Enhanced Partnerships:** Strong relationships can foster partnerships and collaborations.

Effective Follow-Up Strategies:

1. **Create a Follow-Up Plan:** Develop a personalized follow-up plan for each customer, considering their specific needs and preferences.
2. **Stay in Touch:** Regularly reach out to your customers through email, phone calls, or social media.
3. **Provide Value:** Offer more resources, information, or support that can help your customers.
4. **Address Concerns:** Be responsive to any questions or concerns your customers may have.
5. **Seek Feedback:** Ask for feedback on your products or services to identify areas for improvement.

Examples of Follow-Up Activities:

- **Check-in Calls:** Schedule regular check-in calls to see how your customers are doing.
- **Personalized Emails:** Send personalized emails with relevant news or updates.
- **Offer Additional Resources:** Provide added resources, such as whitepapers, webinars, or case studies.
- **Invite to Events:** Invite customers to industry events or webinars.

Referral-Based Sales:

Referrals are a powerful way to generate new business and expand your customer base. By building strong relationships with your customers, you can encourage them to refer you to their network.

Tips for Generating Referrals:

- **Ask for Referrals:** Don't be afraid to ask satisfied customers for referrals.
- **Provide Incentives:** Offer incentives to customers who refer new business.
- **Make it Easy for Customers to Refer:** Provide referral materials and make the referral process as simple as possible.
- **Thank Referrals:** Show your appreciation for referrals by thanking both the referrer and the new customer.

Fact: Referral-based sales usually close at <u>50% to 70%</u> (Sometimes even higher)

By investing time and effort into follow-up and referral-based sales, you can strengthen your relationships with customers, increase customer satisfaction, and drive long-term success.

NOTES:

STEP 14

QUARTERLY BUSINESS REVIEWS (QBRS): STRENGTHENING PARTNERSHIPS

Quarterly Business Reviews (QBRs) are an essential tool for supporting strong relationships with your customers and ensuring their ongoing satisfaction. By conducting regular QBRs, you can gather valuable feedback, identify areas for improvement, and show your commitment to providing exceptional service.

Best Practices for Conducting QBRs:

1. **Use a Standard Format:** Maintain consistency by using a standard format for each QBR. This helps ensure that everyone is focused on the same metrics and forecasts.
2. **Review Action Items:** Start each QBR by reviewing the action items from the previous meeting. This shows your commitment to follow-through and accountability.
3. **Use a Number Rating Scale:** Implement a number rating scale (e.g., 1-5) for specific items such as communication, billing, service, and rep response.

These key indicators can be customized to meet the unique needs of your partnership.

4. **Open and Honest Discussion:** Encourage an open and honest discussion about both the positive and negative aspects of the partnership.

Benefits of Following Best Practices:

- **Improved Efficiency:** Using a standard format and focusing on key indicators can streamline the QBR process.
- **Enhanced Accountability:** Tracking action items and using a rating scale can increase accountability and transparency.
- **Stronger Partnerships:** By addressing issues proactively and showing your commitment to customer satisfaction, you can strengthen your partnerships.

Remember: QBRs are an opportunity to build stronger relationships, gain valuable insights, and drive long-term success. By following these best practices, you can maximize the benefits of QBRs for your business.

That's it for now!

NOTES:

A Word from the Author

Let's cut to the chase. Sales isn't for the timid. It's a ruthless, unforgiving arena where only the strongest survive. If you're not willing to swim in the deep end, you'll be devoured by the competition.

Forget the nine-to-five grind. In sales, your success is directly tied to your predatory instincts and your daily revenue-generating activities. Do you crave luxury, power, and recognition? You've got to hunt for it.

If you're not constantly evolving, you're already becoming extinct. This isn't a leisurely stroll; it's a relentless pursuit. If you're not treating it like a life-or-death struggle, it's time to rethink your career choice.

Managers, stop coddling your sales team. A little fear can be a powerful motivator. Push them to their limits, challenge their every move, and demand nothing short of dominance. If you're not driving them to be better, you're a liability.

Salespeople, it's time to unleash your inner beast. Work tirelessly, sacrifice weekends, and do whatever it takes to close the deal. The playing field is level, but the sharks are hungry. You must be sharper, more aggressive, and more relentless than ever before.

Don't be afraid to strike fear into the hearts of your competitors. Close deals with ruthless efficiency, crush your quotas and become the apex predator of the sales world.

If this message doesn't ignite a fire within you, if it doesn't make you feel a primal urge to conquer, then you don't belong in this game. But if you're ready to dominate, the time is now.

Remember, one day, you may rise to the top of the food chain. When that day comes, pass on this legacy of relentless pursuit. Teach your team that success in sales isn't a gift; it's a hard-earned prize, a testament to their unwavering determination and predatory instincts.

Now go hunt.

Joe Marchese

www.ingramcontent.com/pod-product-compliance
Lightning Source LLC
LaVergne TN
LVHW040951150826
845672LV00002B/644

* 9 7 9 8 8 9 6 9 1 1 6 7 8 *